5 Fingers and 10 Toes

Jo-Jo Goes to School

Copyright 2017 Dawn Civitello.

Published by CreateSpace Independent Publishing Platform

All rights reserved. No part of this document may
be reproduced or transmitted in any form or by any means,
electronic, mechanical, photocopying, recording, or otherwise,
without prior written permission from Dawn Civitello.
For information regarding permission,

email: 5fingersand10toes@gmail.com

Printed in the United States of America

ISBN-13: 978-1977559524
ISBN-10: 1977559522

To my little boy, Jo-Jo.
Be proud of who you are my love,
cause to me you are everything.

Love always,
-Mommy

I said, "No! I don't want to go to school!!"

"What?! Why?!" my mom asked. "I'm scared, I can't even open my lunch box or use scissors!" I shouted.

My mom just stopped and looked at me.

She said, "Don't be silly, you will be just fine."
So we finished up lunch, and off to the mall we went.

We came home with a bunch of new outfits, sneakers, a backpack, even a lunch box.

I just sat there looking at all the new stuff spread out on my bed.

My mom came into my room and saw me sitting there with a worried look on my face.

She said, "Don't be upset buddy, you will be fine, you always are."

That night I couldn't sleep. I was so worried about what my first day of school would be like.

I kept thinking...
What if I can't cut with scissors or paint like the other children.

I also wondered what the children would think of my little hand.

The next morning my mom woke me up for school. I ate breakfast, brushed my teeth, got dressed and walked out to wait for the bus.

When the bus pulled up, Mom gave me a kiss and off I went.

While on the bus, I kept thinking... Will the children like me? What will they think of my little hand?

In my heart, I knew I could do everything they could do, just hoped they could see that too.

When we arrived at school, I lined up with the other children. We walked into a very colorful room and sat on the carpet. Our teacher, Miss Cheryl, said we were going to play an icebreaker game.

To my surprise, it was a game to get to know everyone's name. As we were playing, I saw a boy named Jim looking at my little hand, but he didn't say anything to me. I felt a bit nervous.

After the game, we went to the table to practice coloring and cutting. My heart sank. Miss Cheryl handed out paper with a large square on it. She told us to do our best.

I colored in the lines as my mom had shown me to do. Then held the paper flat with my little hand and began cutting. The girl next to me stopped and stared at me as I cut the square.

The teacher came over to me and said, "Wonderful cutting Joseph!" Turns out, although my way of cutting is different, I cut just as well as the kids in my class.

Lunch time came and Miss Cheryl said, "Get your lunchboxes and take a seat at the table." I felt a bit nervous, but knew I had practiced many times before.

So I sat down held my lunchbox in the crease of my arm and pulled open the zipper without a problem.

After lunch, we had an art project to complete. Miss Cheryl said, "We are going to be making a handprint mural as a class, using paint."

One by one, she went around the room painting and pressing down everyone's hands onto this large piece of paper. It was my turn, she painted my one hand, than asked if it was okay to paint my little hand, I nodded my head "Yes."

After the last handprint, Miss Cheryl held up the mural for us to see. She said, "Look how nicely our first class project came out, we will hang it up once its fully dry."

Jim yelled out, "What happened to that one handprint? It looks so small!"

The teacher stopped and said, "You see one of our friends was born with only 5 fingers." She looked at me, so I stood up and said, "Yes, I was born with only 5 fingers but I am okay and it doesn't hurt me."

Most of all..... "I can do all the things you can do with, my 5 fingers and 10 toes."

Made in the USA
Monee, IL
02 February 2024